rootlines

rootlines

kelsey day

Rootlines, Second Edition
Copyright © Kelsey Day 2021
First Edition Published by Wilde Press, Boston, MA
Trade Paperback ISBN 978-0-578-90141-1
Cover Design by Lucia Gorman
Cover Concept and Illustration by Sadie Hutchings and Nicole Turner
Interior Design by Alea Adrian
Interior Illustrations by Alea Adrian, Sadie Hutchings and Kate Rispoli
Typefaces used are Garamond, Minion Pro, and Tomarik
Printed by Ingram Spark

for appalachia

introduction

In 2018, I published a poetry collection called *the last four years*.

That book is a time capsule of my high school experience—the raw, searing aches of growing up. It was in turns outrageously honest and elusive, dizzy and awkward and confessional. At the time that I published it, I was an anxious high school senior and I was still in the closet. I had just been accepted into a college in Boston and I was leaving my small mountain town in North Carolina to live in the city for the first time.

My creative writing teacher, Stephen Shane, shared a quote from Rainer Maria Rilke that sums up how I've spent the last three years since then: "Be patient toward all that is unsolved in your heart… the point is, to live everything. Live the questions now." My time since publishing *the last four years* has been spent living through every question and grappling with every strange and frightening and hopeful answer. What I have come back to, again and again, is my connection to the earth. To the mountains I come from, that I keep returning to. The roots that give me the strength to grow branches.

What does it mean to be a queer, neurodivergent woman living in the mountains of Appalachia? How is my home being affected by climate change and a carbon-based economy—and how can I stand in solidarity with indigenous groups that have long been fighting to prevent this destruction? What can I do to oppose the violence that is still being committed against the Appalachian mountains?

I don't have any perfect answers. But I've been living through the questions. *rootlines* is the result.

All the profits from copies of this second edition of *rootlines* are being donated directly to the Indigenous Environmental Network. You can donate more at www.ienearth.org. While you're at it, you can read up on the Mountain Valley Pipeline and learn about the destruction it poses to the Appalachian mountains.

Poetry is not activism. This collection is not a solution, but a conversation—a place to start and a place to build from. We are all responsible for doing more. I've included some suggested reading in the back of this book to keep the conversation going.

I'm sending so much love and hope to each of you. Welcome to *rootlines*.

yours in haste,
kelsey day

a little night music

pianissimo
        [very quietly]

we open with a glaring closeness   nocturnal poplars   itching strings.
the folktales arrive anxiously, with their heads down.
impressive, these impulsive and sobbing bloodlines, which twine so softly
beneath the grasses.

accelerando
        [with increasing speed]

consider the slow mechanical pull of the stars, flame ridden and hanging.
the ground, a whimsical ruin. the humans, stirring in their sleep.
layer in the oak blades, quietly at first. follow the conductor: one,
two,   three,   four   one, two, three, four
one two three four   one two three four   onetwothreefour.

con fuoco
        [with fire]

now the fire gapes like an open wound, and we follow the thread
through the skin.
under and in. royal humiliation. key change.
this becomes a furious awakening. you can hear it in the metallic
soprano howl. in the flowering blisters. in the way it hurts
to look.

insectarium

1: *Photinus pyralis*

the grass sizzles, seizes my bare feet, and I
hurtle through the dark with a speed only
children are capable of.
we slam jars over everything that moves,
cradle crawling pulses between our knuckles

2: *Phausis reticulata*

we smell like mud but the bugs don't care
we watch their abdomens unravel, leave
stains in the air   I ask how do they do that
she says light they do it with light
I say where do they get it
she says they make it, they make it with their
bodies   chemicals   communication
I say oh
and we watch the air vibrate with their enzymes

3: *Photinus carolinus*

dad stands by the car, watching the fireflies.
he is angry. not the type of angry that shouts but that watches
he doesn't watch me   he watches the fireflies
water tension   burning leaves   no shouting.
this subfamily of fireflies only appears in the summer
in the appalachian mountains
when someone has betrayed you.
they blink in unison, communicate without
a single syllable
dad watches

4: *Pyractomena*

fireflies live underground in the winter
swimming in larvae, building light in
their bodies   I never see them in the city
but I imagine them waiting   beneath the
concrete, blinking to one another, holding
on until the cavernous summer   reaches its
hand in and spreads its palms   makes a jar
out of
open fingers

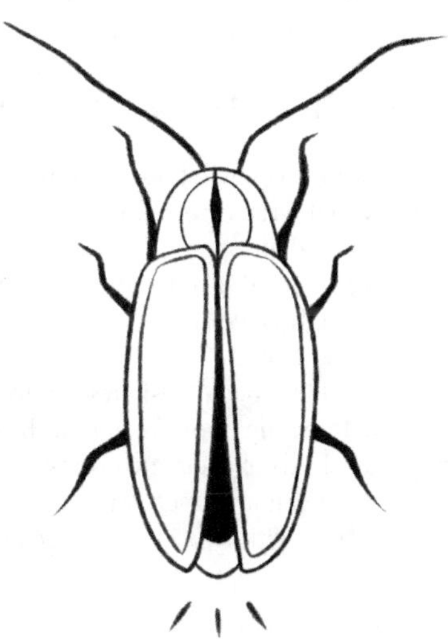

theories

theory: the acorns in my pocket are not seeds but houses
messy fleshy hearts carved into trees by the side of the river.

theory: when I walk through these ancient streets, I am not held by pavement
but by hands,
reaching up from under miles of silt and limestone,
and when I say good morning I mean,
what were you dreaming about? I mean,
where do you go when you slip over
the cliffs of sleep, what pulls you to the surface
at strange silver hours, when I am asleep and
not beside you?

theory: these ghosts are not ghosts
but music boxes,
a history that floats on top of the water.
and when I say I want to fall in love, I mean
I want to be seen—seen like a memory, like déjà vu,
like waking up in the middle of the night, not knowing who I am.

theory: I want to be what pulls you to the surface.
the legacy that wraps around your feet
and holds you drifting.
and a hummingbird is not a hummingbird
but a clock, tightly wound.

theory: when the magic hesitates, so do you—
a nocturnal turning door, frozen on the steps, holding my wrist in october.
and the lazy howl of the metro is my breath, caving in.
and a secret is not a secret but a country,
overpopulated, with its own language and time zone.

theory: you are not a woman
but a premonition,
an ice cube sizzling in my palm,
going out.
and when you say how are you, you mean
what are you
you mean
tell me what
you're made of

of earth:

I wonder if she loved us the day we were born,
blistering and bald out of convulsing dirt, if her
stomach dropped a little at the sight of this
catastrophe she expelled, this reckoning that crawled out of her,
skinless, seething, who opened their eyes and
pinched their lips and
rasped, undaunted:
"more."

may, appalachia

I dream of a car crash, an exorcism, and my old dorm room,
in that order.
The lake fumbles beneath my feet.
My parents hug me goodnight.
A dog snores into my neck.
I dream of overripe lungs, bottomless weeping, and the willow tree in my
          front yard,
in that order.
I eat when I'm supposed to.
I make friends with the walls, the screens, the bed frame.
I feel loved, a thousand times a day.
I dream of a burial, a train ride, and a forest,
in that order.
I make amends with my cells,
to fill the time.
I close my eyes, and I close the window,
in that order.
My hands become sightless widows,
grieving.
I fall asleep, a cellphone tower
softly blinking, ignoring
every coded wail.
I dream of holding my ears in my palms, rusted door hinges, and her
          lemonade mouth,
in that order.
I unhook from my body before falling asleep
dissolve with such unbridled sweetness
     such terror
I hang suspended in the wild and precious dark

virgo moon
Originally Published in Brave Voices

i blink sand out of my eyes/listen to the ancient tides sob.
she sits knees-to-chest/surging, lucid. touching her is a
rapture/i am not ready for.

i fill mason jars with algae and soap/she throws the sea
glass back into the ocean/again and again/until there is
nothing more to soften.

i press my forehead into the tender/violet webs
on my palms/my veins, this casual netting, tossed
overboard wide and swinging.

i try to find something to say/clamber, wingless and
dimming/and still, i don't know/why i never feel so
alone as/when i am loved/loudly.

prerequisite

there is something here from before,
that I forgot in the too warm bed of my mother.
and sometimes I miss being a parasite, I want arms like a cage
and hot milk warmed by somebody else and
I don't want to make my own blood for once.

> I wonder if it moves for me, this
> hallucinated body.
> or if it moves for something else.
>
> I wonder if my skin is still scared of
> disappointing me.
> if my white blood cells
> like the rain.

three sisters trail

I lay traps for juniper. lure the cypress, as the cypress lures me—mutual.
the metal in my jaw pulls taut. I think, *I have known this place.* even
as it buries me. I have seen it in the shards of herkimer, in the stuttering
forest, at the edge of every tripping reflection. I follow the birch roots
underground. perch on boulders. a sagebrush sparrow dives underwater,
and I collect its aching sheen. she reads me a poem about drowning—no,
about the feeling of drowning when you haven't actually drowned, a clock
bursting with thistle, opal littering the creek side. I tie hematite to my wrists
and step into the water. knee-deep, no bottom. I stuff hemlock into lockets,
find a map snagged in a tree. I whisper, hopeless with love. *thank you.*
the wind roars
like she heard me.

decay

meet me in the undergrowth.
where the water (slick. hungry.)
becomes blood, and the blood (rusting. hollow-eyed.)
becomes oil, and the oil (slithering out your mouth, your eyes)
becomes next year's harvest.
where a strapped down creature howls inside your body.
meet me where we are eaten alive,
methodically, with good manners.
where we grow into the leaves,
rotting skin full of song,
meet me in the place between now and after,
where you don't need to forgive anyone
where your body forgives you
where you forgive your body
(for its forgetfulness)
(for the language she never taught you)
(for the how fragile she became, in the end)
meet me where you forget sickness
and become it instead
where you lie with only yourself
and let the insects come

wreckage in the river

I've been building a house.
I sit by the river to work on it,
grateful down to the roots of my teeth,
listening to the stony bank crackle.
I turn stones over in my hands. watch the
juncos glitter. feel how they eye the
seams of me.
this, of course, is to say I have been
building a house,
and so far I have only the floor,
cool wood humming over something like
water. when I press my palms against it
I can just barely feel it vibrating. the birds
circle me, and the water bites at my toes, and
I know, I know, that I too will be weathered
down, eroded into what the water will make of me—
I, another stone, washed over, eyes up.
but I've been building a house and tomorrow,
I will build the walls—and today
I am still
and rooted
beneath the trembling ripples.

dan

in the forests unquiet.
beneath the bark, in the sugared rot.
in the jawbone of a rescue dog.

in sleep talk, foreign languages.
lemongrass in the gutter
grass in your mouth
in hotel bathrooms
crystal blankness
a too-fast heartbeat.

in the unsinking footprint
the stubborn oracle
the brambles we harvest.
all hands, all hope, clumsy
with love.

you deserved another summer.
another day soaked in fog, the mountains
humming against the back of your neck.
another night,
to breathe loudly
even if you couldn't fall asleep.

bristle cone: a conversation

your bristles grow in fives. and the strands don't dance nor latch
into spirals nor push their breath into careful segments—and they
do not tumble free under my clumsy hands.

*(yes, the quartz grows at my
feet. but I am not hungry. I
have nothing to teach you of
hunger.)*

you eat wildflowers with no teeth. chew the light so slowly that
it looks like alchemy. I'm tempted to treat you like an oracle,
half-underground and listening. see the way I press my palms down?
I feel the roots pulsing, a bruising web. what do you have to tell me?

*(vein and root are no
different.)*

I have known vein and root to be
a breathless violence.
I should shed my flesh like a serpent,
tear myself out of my frame.

*(a common mistake, this
notion of separation.)*

vein is not root but rot – a natural undoing.

*(natural is a lie
of human language.)*

I came here with no clocks. empty wrists. legends of perfect timing.
a junco led us up the ridge, hopping over the charred bodies.

*(there are no veins and
no roots. no trunks
and no bodies.)*

I ask for nothing. but I will raise my eyes,
and see the centuries burn.

gently

and yes, i am afraid
in the starch white streets when
my makers try to understand me.
when i miss a moment
before it happens.
i am afraid when
the night treats me gently,
when she reaches
for my rippling skin
and i want to pull her closer.
when the street light clings to fading
belgian walls, and a statue makes me
fall over laughing, i am
afraid when i burn like this.
when i am too happy to speak.

a secret:
yes, i am afraid.
but i can hold this fear.
i can love this fear.
i can hold this fear up
to the light, and
say, "look.
here is proof that
things were wonderful,
once."

the accidental birth of a mouth

you don't remember it being conceived, who
planted these teeth in your womb, who
grew this ferocious creature
in the shape of a daughter,
angry daughter,
spoiled to her center, rotting with rage, you
don't know how
you could have harbored such
a loud secret, don't know how
to cradle a scream, breastfeed the
bloom of acid
in the back of your throat, you
expected powdered sugar on pillowcases, this is
a terrible harvest, this is
a blister in the shape of a girl, this is
a famine in the shape of a girl, this is
downturn and feasting and murder—
this is your shame, personified
this is your daughter,
and she is out
for blood.

field guide for the appalachian summer

a body of water (lakeside, pond, river): singing woman; slick and pulling hands.

carved death stone, no postage: old cycles; safety in the smallness.

empty church: snapping spines; forgiveness, above all else, forgiveness.

a willow tree, mid-sob: redemption; eating light, with your back teeth.

airplanes: a lake folding open and closed; water humming.

the stars: light, unburying itself.

the sunset: light, afraid. exhausted. catching its breath.

bruised, cloaked tree line: absence; hanging on.

ivory rush, returning: endorphins, overheating, skyward.

sunrise: light, resurrected; growing like a bean plant—and for no better reason.

vile heaven

this vile heaven upends
easily.
the weeds grow back
when the sun goes out,
and truth drinks like a leech from the
blackened heat of your mouth—
say it out loud,
if you want.
the volume doesn't matter.
a truth makes
us all into enzymes.
teaches us how to undo one another
disassemble so deliciously
dissolve flesh into sugar, into calories, into
something you can use.
a truth or a seed,
a fruit pit that grows into
your stomach lining
say it out loud,
if you want.
if you believe it.
if you think
you can bear it.

choke out the new things that grow here

framing

mom wants a family picture   one of all of us together kicking
up mulch in the front yard so we   dig through our old
church clothes   rewire our sweaters and
bury each other in pinecones   dead leaves   clay
snarl ourselves into pixels   trap it all in chemical sheen
hang it in the attic   and never look   only know
always   that it's there   that there is clay still
drying on   our chins

baby teeth

i dance in footnote
i feel the root and exile of baby teeth
jars of stones   silk   uprooting.
i am a thousand gods, forgiving each other.
a handful of insects, humming against
            the glass. shedding light like wings.
            hatching, uncurling. forgetting.
i think we are made for the howling and the water,
            always becoming reciprocal energy. always
on course.

monochrome
Originally Published in Please See Me

it starts with the bed / crosscurrents, tidelines / my wrists nailed to the pillow / strangled under the curtains / i am / too feeble to turn on the lights / the laundry sweats in the hamper / rubber bands snap, unsnap / my body becomes aware that it is a body / it knocks on the window / and turns on its side / everything tastes like pennies and i / clutch my stomach cover my mouth i / try to blink the color back into my eyes i / fall asleep in my car by price lake / we used to go on picnics here / the moon is wailing / the ground is wailing / i am wailing and / when i say i am wailing i / mean i am sleeping i / mean i have fallen asleep again i / mean i am possessed by monochrome i / mean i am chronically absent i / mean you must forgive me for this you / must witness this wasteland you / must beg / and beg / for water

recurring dream: a screenplay

EXT. DUSTY SHORES, CRACKLING. DAY.

Sea plants crawl, long-legged, over smooth rocks and tidepools. A house sways in the sand. There is an IVORY SHEEN to the set.

PAN TO:

A series of TENSE DEWDROPS that quiver but never break open. The sun is closer than usual, but the film has the contrast turned down. Everything is pale and rippling.

PAN TO:

A softly cackling path. Shivering coast trees. We can hear CRASHING WATER.

PAN TO:

Her. Hold there.

Hold. Hold. Hold.

SLOW PAN TO:

Me, barely breathing. Barely able to believe my luck.

and I promise

1. that we will crouch in that water again, a choir of fish listening to your finicky splendor. that the nakedness will mean nothing but that we are unafraid. that we will be wild and unmoored in the summer, that it will be hot enough to melt rocks, hot enough to turn the riverbank smooth.
2. that I will forgive the grazing quiet. the slow corrosion of every leaf. the wondrous hollows. every uproot.
3. that I will find you on the creek path, face furiously red. complaining about politics and processed food. pointing at the vultures overhead. insisting that it all means something.
4. that all of this will happen here. not in the brambles, the holy grounds, the tide pools. not in pixels.
5. here.

no sense

we both know this time of morning
doesn't follow the same logic we do.
half-night, here we obey fishing ponds and hollow wells
submit to the logic of wishes.
here, we kiss the blood off our knees.
we ache for blindness,
cradle our blisters like children.
we ache for remembering, for proof of skin
and sweat and cinnamon, the memory
of happy,
tripping over its feet.

here, i beg.
adrift in the machine of memory
here, where i live with and for the past
i beg.
bring me somewhere i know.
bring me somewhere i've been before.
bring me somewhere that hurts
in a way
that is familiar

yes, I still run

and yes, I still run, when april hallucinates gleeful
and your hair sticks in my mouth,
and I fall twenty stories just to tell the story.
yes, I still run, in the migrant ache of an unpacked sun,
tracking time across my shoulder blades,
undressing in the garden before everyone else is awake.
yes, I still run, when I give up my mouth,
and my classes grade my personality,
and I wait in line for an elevator, a train, an airplane.
yes, I still run, when I am lucid in the dark
and taste plums and midnight and know that
I love you,
or me,
or something.
yes, I still run.
when my pillow starts to smell like her.
when the medication starts to work.
when it seems like a good idea
to stick around.

dead language

make a list of terrible things.
every reason you could have left me first.
every reason I've been left before.
squeeze me between a sour note, unharmonize,
call me out of tune, call me
infected with a mortifying light.
make my name a dead language.
a hilted prayer.
an exorcism.

morning

Originally Published in Tipping the Scales Literary & Arts Journal

she reads an unsent letter over breakfast,
speaking around the scorching petals in
her mouth, heady chamomile, lazy threads
of smoke climbing up the windowpane,
humming against the bug screen.
I keep being baptized by this place.
we spread cards over the table. all aces. the
birds are laughing. we can hear the hushed
prayers of the trees outside the window.
I have come to know something fundamental.
smoothies at midnight. a blue screen, gaping.
banana ice cream cooling in our mouths.
You are in good hands.
singing bowls. undrowned streets. you are here,
and so am I.
So be it.

and how can I grieve

with these envelopes I find tucked under sea stones, and the picnic table
softly smoking—when the fog is friendly, sniffing my hand like
a childhood dog and the cliffs hug me to their chest and I call my mother
       and
the strings snap tuneless, dripping sap and gold, how can I grieve when I
cannot come home, when I will not come home, when it feels so urgent to
worship, to go blind with gratitude, to snarl back into a seed,
how can I grieve when my body is a thousand miles away already and the
       branches
are bleeding out of my crown, no thorns, how can I grieve when death is
       not
something that happens to me but with me, when my skin is still knotted
       and my
blood is still harsh and still loud, and I don't even believe it yet, how can I
       grieve
when you are gone and the world is still ringing in my ears, when every
       echo still
sounds like an echo, when I trip over my own love and land on my hands
       and knees
and the dirt smears into my palms and the blood rushes to my head and I
       feel the earth's
heartbeat hot and dry and pricking and I think it sounds like heaven, and I
       think it sounds like
       you

afterlife

I put my clumsy hands in other people's pockets.
think,
this is what death would be like, if
death was any good.
this unshakable closeness.
this oversaturation.
this most tender
uproar.

she/they

I won't ask to be looked at out loud.
or admit to the stilted rush of

leo's frantic needlework, even when I'm
dead weight in the woods behind

my parents' house, obsidian lodged
between my eyebrows. I forget at times

that I am still an avatar   a feathered
mist, a darling mismatched

construction site. there's no sense in
contorting constellations across graph points

and no, orion's belt still doesn't fit, but
I shimmer in the trying. don't tell me I'm

inconsolable. tell me I'm vast, unbuilt.
a splendid   approximation.

sugar pill

I try to dive, make my body an arrowhead,
but I land on my hands and knees, my body
dented into prayer just before it hits the
water. bland as a sugar pill and half as strong,
I wake up into   (give me a break)
a dream that   (or at least a place to land)
stands on stilts and looks at me,
and I forget every language from every life,
I forget how to refill because
I don't remember absence.

and I think they might nail me to a leather chair in
the hopes that I bleed out, but
I'll eat dust by the handful, stuff
hair in my pockets for later
nothing strange about it
I'll lose my mind just so I can try to find it
misplace every memory, thumb jutted on another planet
there's no structure to this
no need for proof or memory,
but I can feel it stirring,
I can feel its gutted wings, rushing

I am my own daughter

middle child, born in a circle of stones
november fever, flooded riverbanks
let this be a stormless collision
too impatient for chronology
let this be a jasmine brine, creeping
up telephone poles by the side of the highway
miles from the ocean, let this be
a clock with no hands, only
one long and
unlocked stare

and if I'd like to sink

hands wasted, I think
color must be made out of water here,
the water made of hummingbirds
a restless language, an island
where shoulders hitch against shoulders, share
breath and feet and bridges
with other tourists.
no fire, weather grows underground
we call this
a catastrophic drifting
a sinking song, sung backward,
sweat-burned begging
let me go, let me go, let me go.

hunting grounds

mouths grow at the end of branches,
they quirk into a smirk
at the sight of this unrooted being, crashing
through the foliage,
eye me through the sockets of a deer skull.
drop acorns, tilt crowns
I vibrate and clatter, messy thing
feigning inheritance
wonder how many downed giants
I must crawl over
to make it back to pavement,
how much of me will be left
when the leaves and the mouths retract
what makes the green flesh push through its casing,
what slow unfolding
I still have
in me

places i wish i haven't hidden

1. i always leave the table first/stand up too fast and/hide in the pearly
    blindness/easy to love/hard to get along with/i sink into the backwash
    blindness like water/feet over my head/floating like a winged seed/
    never landing

2. in the glass hook/on the porch breathing in/out/waiting for the lights
    to turn on

3. another human being/i run my hands along the ridges until i find a
    grip/until i find a place to/infiltrate/and take root/when i come looking
    for me/i'll be safely nestled/under someone else's skin/i'll hold my
    breath/as she walks by

4. small spaces/where i can feel my breath rattle/like frustrated wind/
    wardrobes/cabinets/car trunks/eyes open drinking dark/sweat behind
    my ears/no speaking

5. in plain sight/red shoes and trembling strings, july/more of an aesthetic
    than a human/coming into focus the farther/and farther/you walk
    away

crossing over

she speaks in bodies of cold water
language a mouthful of salt and current
and I visit this place even when
I am not here, even when I am
sunk in sleep in the gray mountains
I return here, to this relentless
way of speaking, a rock skipping across
flooded banks, red clay unrolling, I still
slip into ancient tongues, to the
oldest way of saying,
I am here,
with you,
now

diving board

feet first
(only seeing if)
arms out like
(this could be different, if)
there's a place to land like
(this place can do anything other than swallow me whole, if)
there's something different waiting like
(there's more to this than jumping, if)
i can collapse and call it
(fleeing   roaring   landing)
creation

ants

ants settled into the walls while I was gone.
I pull back my bedcovers and find their legs, fluttering
frothing chemical trails all the way back to boston.
I leave them peppermint and vinegar,
watch them twitch and die on the carpet, looking up at me.

I read that killing one ant is like clipping a fingernail
I find their body parts in the pantry
homeless abdomens and bait, candied
like orange vitamins, like dissected spirits,
a nuisance.

I infest this homeland with
missing legs with
warm ginger poison with
trembling gutters, rooftops that
can't hold the weight of an insect that
can't hold the weight of
a fingernail, tugged from its cell stitchings,
ringed with wingless red, watched
closely like
it might plan something, like
it might sink another trail in, like
it doesn't matter if the food is poisoned
because all it wants
is to bring
something
home

dominion
Written in Protest of the Atlantic Coast Pipeline

it starts underground. the mountains choke up bile and
orange peels grow out of the sand like fingers. the
rivers crackle into flame, wail for matches, the water
holds bottles like floating bodies on the surface
oil buzzing in the water, oil writhing in our mouths, oil
squeezed between the cracks in our teeth, copperheads twined
around toddlers, we float on the water with the grease
admire the churning colors, and does a forest really fall if
we make enough money if we make enough money, if we
write over their bodies, make it into a well-oiled machine
copy-paste axes into temples, hair torn from scalps
unrotting collapse terrible musical dying, and does a forest
really fall if our bodies corrode into coin, dissolve into
sand, grow orange peels like fingers? if our bodies press
into metal press into axes press into temples press into press
into press into press into press into press into press into press—

make me a birdhouse

peeled strawberries   hangnails stinging   compost
a sparrow burrows in my palm
makes a birdhouse out of quiet hands
no feathers, no wishbone
        (i suddenly know what it is, to hide a self
        inside a self inside a self inside a self
        each one keeping a secret from the other)
the rings in the granite eat itself
a snake digests its belly
surface smooth as ice
        (i become duality upending motion
        landing on my hands and knees
        soft as a blackberry petal
        in someone else's mouth)
box cutters   fissured wallpaper   bars of soap
this honeyed sparrow roars in the dogwood
hangs from the underside of bridges
        (and i think when my body snaps
        like a secret, when i leak out
        of these hands and recycle to dirt
        again, i would like to be
        buried in birdseed)

bread & wine & the body

i'm lucky—
for me, it was never about the calories   it was about the body
about the blood baked into the dough   the sins and spices, tickling my throat
wine a sip of death   food, a slow and musical dying

earthly pleasures

the machine hum of the south.
a hammock slowly swinging.
breakfast.
a tangerine that could sit in a teaspoon.
taking off my bracelets.
talking to myself, telling myself stories that sound like prayers.
collecting rocks in the backyard
in my underwear.
dogwood petals unraveling
buttercup smeared under my chin
trading memories with my sister.
childhood logic, unmade beds
the smell of my own sweat
the smell of dog fur and allergies.
creaking docks. low flying airplanes that
I wave to,
despite everything.

serpentine

she crams a snake in a jar, hides it
in the fridge next to the apple juice and butter.
serpentine curls in maple water, suspended
mouth peeking open,
no fangs.
she tells no one.
after dark, she visits him in
flannel pajamas when
her parents have gone to bed.
she asks it to help her fall asleep.
she asks it why it gives birth between its eyes.
she asks if it can ever forgive her for
her tender childlike violence,
for her need for proof,
for all the living secrets she has crammed into jars, to save
and look at later.

projection

I wrap my arms around the sweet rot, press my cheek into the tree's
buckling lungs, its curdled bark, and breathe—*god*—breathe—*I'm here, I'm
listening*—breathe—*who are you? what is this*—breathe.
until the aspen opens its eye.
until the blue columbine meets me halfway.
until the nocturnal angels rise from the hot wet earth and drag me under,
again.

obituary

public notice: she has slipped back into
the water. the current is strong. it knows
the way.

thirst

I burrow in the pollen, sun bobbing up and
down in my throat, heartburn squeezing
like an animal underground
I raise walls of sandpaper to bounce off
the ravenous fever, I
fall asleep along vertebrae of brail and
gaps in the hardware
> (I have a dream about vanilla coke, the
> metallic snap and my tongue unfastening)
> (I have a dream about the wetlands, how we
> dig up lightbulbs and drink ice out of their
> gaping mouths)
> (I have a dream about desert birds, see them rave
> in wide moaning circles overhead, waiting for my knees
> to crumple)

three sisters swamp: an alternate timeline

my friend almost drove off a bridge and so
we met up at the three sisters swamp, me
and the two girls I love, and we all slid into
the mouth of cape fear, think pirates and
bike grease and snakes falling out of trees and
praying with knees digging into marsh stones
and sweat curdled under your earlobes and love
eating into you like mosquitoes, tiny teeth shrieking
visions, a two-thousand-year-old tree, a water
god crouched and asking, of all people, for us.
(we wake up without drowning.)
(the view nearly kills us.)

mill creek

a five minute walk from our campsite there is a dead god, half-buried,
and its body is too wide to wrap my limbs around, so i climb into its lap
and stretch. lying flat across the stump, neither my hands nor feet touch
the outlines. though dead, this god vibrates, quietly. i feel its shivers hot
through the moss and insects, humming against my ribs. there is a ring of
new trees encircling the fallen father. they watch me, ancestor of axes. they
watch me. brie says she's never seen a dead thing breathe. she presses her
palm flat against the rings in the wood. we listen to it breathe. feel its chest
      rise
and fall. the sunlight falls in paper slants between the children's shoulders.
      they
watch me, the circle tightening. they watch me. no anger. they watch me.
      no fear.
as if these children can see the fallen trees inside of me. as if they knew all
      of their names.

what I would tell you, if you were here:

1. the mountains are flooding. it is night. the sky is a dark wine, unspooling.
2. I weave water into jars. I fill my mouth with soil. I hide under the bed from lightning.
3. my feet know me better than anyone. I am learning that I must trust them.
4. I cannot sleep unless my ears are pressed to the earth. I cannot sleep until I go mad with listening.

father's day

green hands earth, rotting red clay a mouthful of amber oak leaves:
he worries. worries for the water for the birds that die of grief
for every snake and baseball every writhing beast in the sand

he loves his world in sweeping strokes of worry, his eyes a tender
knot, a troubled gardener a field poet, queasy with love, this
aching gardener grows us like a magic trick, we hungry saplings.

a few times a year, all his plants grow in the same direction—to him
the ivy curls clockwise, and the flowers bend in his direction, the trees
bow their heads, and carolina creek beds surge and roar, and he just sort
of looks bewildered, grinning, a gardener gaping at the love he grew

library card & driver's permit

bitten paper   husks   naked feet
slick dirty roads, standing shoulder to shoulder
at the top of a waterfall   holiday blues
stereo cackling   snake holes   years, unspooling from
one another   all of this   all of us
a tangle   too magnificent   for unwinding

fraser

I lie down by the river and let the crows tear into me.
they warble old hymns as they twist between my ribs,
rose quartz impatient in their beaks. they track my seams
and ridges while I lie clutching feathers in sweat-slicked
fists, afloat in a trust so sharp that it has become soft again,
under a sun so bright it has become dark again, a sphere
of black, a raging glow, pinpricks and messengers, and I am
screaming with my mouth closed, I am sobbing with my
eyes torn out, come in, come in, *come in*—

mesa trail, october

these are the moments I question my biology:
my throat, threaded through a pine needle
my vertebrae, unlocking between the tree teeth
while the crickets throb, insects sweating
pinpricks in the soil.
october clogs my ears: a wordless upheaval.
and what is the wind but a heavenly butcher, a blood-cut
gasp in the ponderosas—
I lie down next to the body.
the grass comes up to my eyes, yellow in the smoke.
and what am I but a tourist in the burning.
peeling bark off my skin in flakes and chewing it into soil.
what am I but another snapped moth, wings like an
unhinged jaw. a surrender of acute angles. bile and
strawberries. what am I but another knee pressed into
earth-shards. hands pressed together not in prayer
but in witness.

echo location

the swamp swallows its own echo/the long sleeves and lanky roots
flaying the/softly whirring copies/we stand over the door and
hum like choir thieves/lucid in the winter solstice/I cling to my
sister as she dips headfirst/into the ink that beats like blood/like
a head rush/vision loose and unraveling, she stares/says she/
doesn't see it/says, hanging like a bat/in the rustling mirror/eyes
wild with dark/that she doesn't see/anything/at all—

(says that she had a dream
that she drove her car into
this river, water filling her
windows and ears, the
headlights stretching arms
through the burnt water,
that she was sinking, that
she was alone in the
crowding currents, that she
was afraid, that she was
so
afraid)

retelling

—and the sky was this infinite comfort, planted firmly against my lapping vision—my neck pressed into dead leaves, the woods rushing—me, an ice chip in the wind's mouth, a searing dissolution—I slept there until the day became ancient—until my bones hugged armfuls of dirt several feet below, chin still tilted up—famously unconscious—trembling at the way this body held onto me, despite—every act of treason—every attempt to leak out—I lay there in the bramble, asleep—each drowsy breath—an affectionate terror—

mirroring

draining flight, ankles arched over my head
twenty-two feet underwater
the nettles around my neck do not wilt in the devouring softness

my shoulders green and cursive, I am
made for erosion, and here everything is
unspeakably close

there is no bottom to this water, only another
surface to break,
a parallel sky to gasp from
rise, child, rise—

I emerge from the creek bed a
bewildered tourist

I emerge from the crawl space a
half-eyed prophet, one foot in the water

duke energy

Originally Published in Storm Cellar Literary Journal
Written in Protest of the Atlantic Coast Pipeline

we clamber over the fence on/a cold mountain night in july, moon washed down our backs/ankle-deep in the stream, oil clots/breaking apart our sentences, we/dip black water into mason jars, milkweeds drowned beneath the metal lids/fireflies writhe under the surface, choking/we don't collect them/we put ivy under a microscope, study its half-grimace/how it flinches from our fingers/we flee from the satellites/bury our bodies in warm sour hay, the horses howling/rivers tunnel down our streets, down our/bones, oil ribbons unrolling, blood spitting in the pan/we cough petals into wilting hands/pay our bills with baby teeth/dig parasites out of our gas tanks/drizzle gasoline over chamomile petals/sit in the dark, not touching/ waiting for the/lights/to come on

your most toxic trait and why

when I was a kid, I lived for the floods.
most days I woke up already ankle-deep,
my skin wilting and sour, mouth relentless,
reaching out with light-sucked fingers to
coax the same out of my allies.
I ate secrets without chewing—found
a dead child's ring, hands braced against shoulders,
a bottle of blue circles—and woke up for the first
time craving sand. call it a conversion. a migration.
a mutiny, the sting of anger I feel when you are
good to me. comfort-starved and biting.
no wind, no wells. sand itching under eyelids.
now I make conversation into a burial
ache for the simplicity of violence
wake up with dirt in my mouth
hands over my ears
fists between teeth
I make an empty room out of me
I ask all the right questions
I drift, landlocked,
unanswerable

after

the slow-turning petals smell like
corrosion, the hushed urgency of ancient kindling, the
act of burying
              and reburying
                    and reburying
                          and reburying.

I seal my eyes with sap.

I forgive her with sand draining into my mouth.

lake voices

listen closely. you, in the reeds.
crouched in the caves that fill with water.
moon-flung and delirious, we watch you
wither, unfounded.

        —yes, I scrape the algae off my elbows,
        and I can't make a language out of the ripples,
        no matter how unsettling. am I supposed to
        be ashamed of that?

in the gutted shadows, bent twenty
feet below, I am asking for some focus.
some attention to these unsettling ratios.

        —the act of a human birth is an act of fleeing
        water.

but don't you miss the drifting?

        —I am trying to say that I don't believe in an
        unselfish thirst.
        only a hard and restless need
        to avoid the burning

there is no burning here. only
time to sit and
watch the water rise.

winter solstice

phone weeping fissures
tender gasoline
the number four, glitching
seams and glitter, what we
came to see has already drifted
below the outline, this ancient
blushing closeness, a helpless
conjunction eight hundred years arriving,
but we sit at the ley line anyway,
balance blankets over our heads,
clutching wind-cracked hands over
the simmering mugwort.

the candle is a pupil, blinking
tiger's eye and hematite.
we breathe together
while the wind roils delighted
it's past twelve when our feet
go numb, and I make the others
wait by the car while I
strip in the half-full dark
climb beneath the blinding waters,
every cell a
magnificent surrender—

bitch you're crazy

biting the filter of her cig, half naked in
the back seat, windows gaping. she laughs.
I bury my head in a stranger's lap,
smell her smoke like a light at the
end of the hall, the simplest type of
witness

god I love you

waffle house, holy and glowing. the witch's choice.
my backpack, clanging with mason jars   stones   cords—
I never knew it could be this easy, communing
with holy terror. making peace with
the drowning.

translation of the rivulets left by a bronze birch borer:

this is the lie: that you can be anywhere but
sputtering in a filthy curiosity.
floating on your back while every
unkempt mouth drains summer out the
splinters—
how primitive it is,
to have a heartbeat.

burial

they buried me so lovingly/in the encrypted hayfields.
blind and thrumming/I watched the decomposition

watching me, still twitching/with an incurable reluctance.
the bacteria settled quickly, limbs multiplying/patient with the

disgruntled signals, the body's/fatal hope. immune to
these eyes unblinking/the simplicity of a failing code.

remember it is nothing personal/this impulsive burial.
this dirt, crawling in your nostrils/this senseless wanting.

i found heaven and it is a circle

I lift my hands in hallucinated light,
sending love through the rootlines.
letting it out of my skin, a little.
letting the space bite me.
trusting the spark of blood, of heat, of tender desperate living.

believing in
whatever place this is.

rootlines

beneath the urgent floods
the honeyed stones and braids of chrysalis
beneath the nest of wild grass and shed talons,
the churning beasts are not sleeping.
I spot them on a walk with my family.
my body rushes to fill itself.
roots rumble under the pavement, snarling bike chains
catch between my fingers—see the bent paperbacks, the
flecked lenses, the plunging shortcuts through the trees—
a woman, praying at the rootline.
a spirit, swallowed in metal, speaking.
saying,
        I am not the last of my kind.
saying,
        I am not the last of anything.

acknowledgements

I'm so grateful to have a wide network of people who made *rootlines* possible. I'm incredibly indebted to the whole team at Wilde Press, especially the fearless publisher Nicole Turner and art director Alea Adrian.

Brianna Cunliffe and Megan Busbice have been my creative best friends since we were teenagers in the hazy Carolina summer. These two women have pushed me, again and again, to be the best person and the best writer that I can be.

My parents and my siblings: you are what home means to me. Thank you for always welcoming me back to the mountains.

Mimi, you will always be my favorite storyteller. Thank you for entrancing me with words from such a young age. Thank you for all those hours on the phone and all those slices—yes, slices—of ice cream.

Maya, Sadie, Lauren, Chloe, and Olivia: thank you for riding every high and low with me. Thank you for every brain break and deep breathing exercise. Thank you for making me feel at home in the city.

Andri, Rebecca, and Keanna: you woke me up that summer by the river. I will never forget it, and I will never forget you.

The poems in this book are based in place. It's therefore essential to recognize that Appalachia as we know it today has been built on stolen land. You can donate to the Indigenous Environmental Network at www.ienearth.org and broaden your knowledge with some of the suggested reading below.

American Sunrise by Joy Harjo

An Indigenous Peoples' History of the United States by Debbie Reese and Jean Mendoza

A Third University is Possible by la paperson

Braiding Sweetgrass by Robin Wall Kimmerer

Green is the New Red by Will Potter

KELSEY DAY is a writer, environmental activist, and mental health advocate from southern Appalachia. Her work is urgent, timely, and relentlessly vulnerable, and has been published in literary journals such as *Reservoir Road Literary Review, Storm Cellar Literary Magazine, Brave Voices Magazine,* and *Our Shared Memory Collective.* She is a recipient of the University of Chicago's Young Memory Fellowship and is an honors student at Emerson College. She works with women from across the globe with the International Women's Writing Guild, is a staff writer for Two Story Melody, and serves as the Head Poetry Editor for *The Emerson Review.*

Publisher
Nicole Turner

Marketing Department
Marketing Director
Andrew Taets
Marketing Assistant
Olivia Lusk
Marketing Associates
Alea Adrian   Kathleen Nolan
Annika Berggren   Anne Rinaldi
Emma Shacochis

Design Department
Art Director
Alea Adrian
Design Manager
Ana Hein
Design Assistant
Lucia Gorman
Design Associates
Sadie Hutchings   Kate Rispoli
Kasey O'Connell   Nicole Turner

Associate Publisher
Olivia Smith

Editorial Department
Head Editor
Madeline Harrant
Assistant Editor
Caja Leshinger
Associate Editors
Sadie Hutchings   Sarah Perry
Andrew Taets

Production Department
Proofreader
Kasey O'Connell
Head Copyeditor
Charlotte Drummond
Assistant Copyeditor
Anna Phillips
Associate Copyeditors
Allison Armijo   Audrey Labonte
Lainy Demeropolis   Hancine Mok
Brianna Jackman   Natalie Obedos
Karina Jha   Gwen Plotner